# X·E·N·I·A

## OTHER BOOKS BY COLEMAN BARKS

**Poetry**

*The Juice*
*New Words*
*We're Laughing at the Damage*
*Gourd Seed*

**Rumi translations**

*Night and Sleep* (with Robert Bly)
*Open Secret*
*Unseen Rain*
*We Are Three*
*Delicious Laughter*
*These Branching Moments*
*This Longing*
*Like This*
*One-Handed Basket Weaving*
*Feeling the Shoulder of the Lion*
*Birdsong*
*Say I am You*
*The Essential Rumi*

**Other translations**

*Naked Song* (Lalla)
*Stallion on a Frozen Lake* (6th Dalai Lama)
*The Hand of Poetry* (5 Persian mystical poets)

# X·E·N·I·A

*A*
*Hoard*
*of Lost Words,*
*Eighteenth-Century Street Lingo,*
*and*
*A Few Completely Confabulated*
*Terms*
*Collected and Exemplified*
*by*
COLEMAN BARKS

Maypop · Athens

MAYPOP
196 Westview Drive
Athens, GA 30606
1-800-682-8637

for tongues

## Boustrophedon

There's a dementia where a person says single words as handholds to climb, spiraling up the inside of the silo of consciousness, and there's freefall when the storage cylinder funnels into the lips of an hourglass open at both ends. Some grain becomes bread, some bird, some dirt, some new cross-pollinated plants. Words travel in various ways, scout out to the side and ahead and bring back bewilderment to our circle of ignorance. Language holds on to ways of thinking and feeling that may seem quaint now, or amazing, or full of longing.

I've never taught a class that didn't, when asked, admit to having precognitive dreams, telepathic incidents, out-of-body experiences, visions, at least half of them, usually more, so why is not this acknowledged part of our lives more studied by science and more welcomed into language? Whitehead once compared Latin to a tight, closed, neatly packed suitcase and English to one lying open with all its contents splayed out.

This sloppy charisma is what I love about English. I want to encourage its undersea dance. Nothing should be left out, experience drunk, sober, waking, half-waking, deep sleep, mysticism, skepticism, experience terrified, carefree, normal, abnormal. Every mode must be accommodated in the search for who and what for and where we are that is language.

The god of the cave in Les Trois Frères is an early and magnificent attempt to write the pronoun mystics so love. You. In a dream once the family, brother, sister, children, their children, were hilariously turning to dust, a vented breeze of our ancestors, we were becoming that, already were, in a closed-in elevator-place, and it was very funny, how what we thought we were was now a rush of particles.

At twelve, thirty-four, and now fifty-six, I have made lists of loved words. Two twenty-two year intervals. I remember the black pop-open ring notebook that kept my first hoard, and a few of the words: *azalea, halcyon, jejune.* For the oddness and the sweetness. Also images unattached to anything: a boy stirring a spiderweb with a stick, the sound of a screen door slamming in summer. This was 1949 in Chattanooga. In 1971 my parents died within six weeks of each other of unrelated reasons, and I dove into the *OED* as I once discovered *underwater* as a mystical inward region for refuge and play, and for some sense that I was reaching through veils into grief and spirit. I published a chapbook, *New Words,* from that submarine swimming. This now is something different. The potter Dennis Parks calls himself a ceramic compulsive. He's unashamedly fanatic about clay, the many textures and properties. He tests them with his tongue. Words are that tasty and tactile, as well as aural and gracile to the eye. I confess to some weird elation for phrasing definitions and stacking them in a list.

Cormac McCarthy's ruined and luminous fisherman, Suttree, one night on his houseboat hears gospel music coming softly from the fillings in his teeth and is "stayed in a peace that drained his mind, for even a false adumbration of the world of spirit is better than none at all." Cormac uses words found in no dictionary but this one. Shakespeare and Joyce did that too. And I have to admit, I have heard music from nowhere. Choral singing, overreaching, inhuman, oceanic voices, and threading up through them a back-country Appalachian hymn, sewing together people with spirit. This was waking and so clear I walked outside the cabin to see if, inexplicably, the Stuttgart Symphony Chorus were not camped nearby. Ruined and luminous, I came back in, sat still, and listened.

I was a stammerer as a child and on into high school, and that probably made the taste of words on my tongue more dear. There was the moment when I became one in Second Grade, Miss Killinger's class, sitting in a circle reading *The Weekly Reader*. My turn, the sentence, a news item, began with *tuna fish*. I could not explode it out, nothing, the silence of my canned-fish self. Now the lovely multi-orgasmic explosions flowering and fluting through the throat. That terror of embarrassment with the word unable to be spoken climaxed in a farcical moment when I was battalion commander and supposed to say, "COMPANY COMMANDERS TAKE CHARGE OF COMPANIES AND MARCH THEM INTO THE CHAPEL," and couldn't, finally waving my sabre in surrender, the commandant lying out on the cement plinth behind me, laughing. Somewhere there is a battalion that never went to chapel. Then women, night-swimming, and the flood gate opening. Song. Thomas Wolfe and Dylan Thomas and Wordsworth. I do want my word's worth.

The collections of my youth: stamps and

postcards and logos cut out of magazines. Creekrocks and feathers, arrowheads and elaborate bugs, the mystery of outdoors. Tony Heywood and I drew floor plans of an infinitely expanding estate, hundreds of floors, museum for the riches of inner and outer. Not greedy, kids' conglomerations are Whitmaniac and generous, exciting as the stereopticon, secret as a crystal radio. With surely sexual longing drenching everything. I dedicate this gangly mansion to that in everyone, with windows some ancient presence gazes from inside, through to wonder and touch. My whole family loves to salvage broken things and find other uses for them. A discarded bus token machine becomes a lamp. A 1927 Buick wheel with wooden spokes reappears as a low table for the hearth.

Words slide away and die and get spoken back to being, or never were, but find picturing, the lion-man-horse-dove fourteen feet up in the dark. Call him *owalag,* a gryllic mix. Engraved, we're still cemetery rubbings, kiddos.

There's a long, bestringed and whirring, greenhouse where, in a sylvan bottomland, someone is tending plants thought extinct for centuries, odd purple broccoli, dwarf carrots, blue-flowered chickweed, always in motion in the warm moist light. Everything is moving, to the eye and within itself.

American Indians have ceremonies for honoring the varieties of corn. It's important to preserve a lot of them, so that when a blight hits one, it won't affect the food supply disasterously. Variety is more than spice. It's how the flooding plays at being numerous. The feel of that sportive presence. Praise for the way host and guest tease and toss conversation back and forth.

> The whole world, says
> Kabir, rests in your play,
> yet the player remains unknown!
>
> — KABIR

The difference between a word and the right word is the difference between a lightning bug and lightning.

> — MARK TWAIN

# Contents

# X·E·N·I·A

*cantabank* — a pretentious ballad-singer, a stage-poet of false emotion.

*cantabile* [KAHN-TAHB-EEELAY] — in a smooth style, suitable for singing. *«The program was relentless cantabank cantabile.»*

*chevalure* — a fancy word for hairdo, the helmet-shape of a woman's head and hair. Also, it means the trail of a comet. *«She walks her chevalure across the night, trailing sparks.»*

*cicisbeo* [SISISBEEOH] — a bachelor cavalier attendant upon a married woman, or a piece of ribbon tied to a sword hilt or ornamental walkingstick as might be carried by such. From a playful reversal of the Italian *belcece,* "beautiful chickpea." *«The feeling on the porch among the three was Jamesian, the early middle years, pure cicisbeo.»*

*homoousian* — from the medieval Latin for Jerome, the saint who knew that the Father, Son, and Holy Ghost were made of the same stuff. Consubstantial with others. *«He called her. She called him, who knows. They sat in their homoousian bath.»*

*incunabula* — a Latin plural referring to books produced before 1500, before the printing press, *cunabula,* swaddling clothes, *cuna,* cradle. Anything in that early time still draped in innocent glory and self-soiling. The breeding grounds of certain species of birds are incunabula. *«All the gospels are silent about his life from twelve to thirty. The meditation masters of India may have been Jesus' real incunabula.»*

*intervital* — being between two lives or stages of existence. Tennyson talks of "the intervital gloom," but every phase seems intervital. *«Isn't the initiatory radiance of now always intervital?»*

*jerque* — to search a ship to see if all the items are duly registered on the bill of lading. *«The IRS man sat at his grey-green desk and jerqued my grocery sack of receipts.»*

*jesse* — a genealogical tree showing the line
of descent of Jesus involving Jesse
the father of David. The fourteen
generations from Abraham to David,
the fourteen from David to the
Babylonian exile, and the fourteen
from the exile to Joseph, the husband
of Mary of whom was born Jesus. *«A
jesse decorated the east window under the
figure of Mary.» «Jesse, jesse, stand up,
jesse!»*

*juba* — a dance done by African-Americans
on plantations during slavery
involving the clapping of hands and
the patting of thighs and the striking
of the floor with feet, as well as a
refrain in which the word *juba* is
frequently repeated. *«Here were the
Virginia slaves clapping juba over a
barrel of persimmon beer.»* Supposedly
unrelated to *jubilee,* from the Hebrew
for the ram's horn used to announce
a year of great forgiveness and
remission and the release of all slaves.
Every fifty years, it says in *Leviticus,*
there was to be a jubilee blast of
trumpets.

**kneeify** — to connect the toe of a shoe to the knee with a light chain attached to a ring just below the knee joint, as was the custom in the 14th Century. *«The kneeified gentlemen made quite a jangle descending to the dancefloor.» «The neophyte kneeified himself for lunch. He felt very fancy.»*

**labascency** — the state of sliding and tottering and wavering down. *«Your sweet labascency wrapped me as I began to lose interest in the movie.»*

**liege poustie** — a Scottish phrase, literally meaning a powerful faithfulness. The state of being in fine health and complete possession of one's faculties. *«Enjoying the news, he walked from the house to the little restaurant in more than* compos mentis, *in full liege poustie.»*

**loneling** — a single child. *«Just the one ah the poor loneling, do suck longer at the breast than the litter pups, do the loneling, the him, the her, whatever it is there. Come here loneling, ye lost soul.»*

**lorate** — shaped like a strap. *«Lorate, her father's shadow fell across the rug.»*

*limous* — of the nature of mud, slimy. *«Sand and limous matter covered the floor.»*

*mysophobic* — a fear of healthy soup, no, a fear of dirt or defilement. *«Mysophobic, he was not.»*

*pulsant* — rhythmically expanding and contracting.

*pulpament* — a mass of food composed of the pulp of plants and / or animals. *«The leftovers dissolved the lesser into the greater to provide one chylous pulpament that no one wanted.»*

*chylous* — from *chyle,* a thick white or pale yellow fluid consisting of lymph and finely emulsified fat produced in the intestine during digestion. The Greek *chylus* means juice.

*prink* — to adorn oneself with petty ornaments. *«The generals sat solemnly in a line garishly prinked about the bosom with campaign ribbons.»*

*pulka* — a Lappland sled shaped like just the front half of a boat and pulled by a single reindeer. *«Lars crested the hill grinning like a miraculous wreck that didn't know it had already happened, his pulka bright blue and green and red against the snow.»*

*pulsatilla* — the shaking of a flower in the wind. *«A gentle pulsatilla riffled the thirdgraders as their teacher appeared on stage.»*

*reeraw* — a confused noise of loud laughter and singing, or like that. *«His reeraw disposition suspended Robert's Rules of Order and made the faculty meetings tolerable.»*

*rigsby* — a prowling, romping, out-for-anything young lad or lassie. *«Four rigsby androgynes turned and took the street as viking galleys must have once appeared to Orkney shepherds.»*

*rike* — to reign, from Old Norse. *«Ere lang the shaman riked a further region beyond my blue dream.»*

*rictus* — the gaping of a mouth. «*In the silent rictus of the television screen the Challenger veered and began dismantling.*»

*sarcel* — a long wingfeather from a hawk. «*His short sketches were plastic imitations of the wild sarcel Chaucer dropped.*»

*sarcle* — to weed with a hoe. «*Uncle Sarcle is at it again.*»

*silique* — a long seed pod. «*In the photograph a curved silique hung just above her head like an accidental Damocles.*»

*skice* — to run and cut quickly, to frisk about like squirrels in Spring. «*The children skiced around the yard, then faded to the grass. Skice and fade.*»

*skibbet* — a closed compartment in the top of a sea chest. «*My grandfather kept his fishhooks in a skibbet where we couldn't find them.*» «*The spleen is a kind of skibbet in the torso full of chemical memories.*»

*venatorial* — connected with hunting, and more precisely, addicted to the chase. *«He belonged to that social class in the South that is strongly venatorial, even canine under its polish, with wives name of Booger and Hootie.»*

*verulamian* — performed by or emanating from Francis Bacon, Lord Verulam. *«Our experiments still accept the verulamian limits on knowledge.»*

*vervecine* — sheeplike. *«Do not respond to their vervecine applause.»*

*vituline* — of or resembling a calf.

*waught* — to drink down in great gulps. *«They waught and waught more till their eyes grew vituline and they sang their vituline songs.»*

*conchology* — the study of shells and shellfish. *«His old love for the sarengi woke, and he fell deeper into meditation like some daring conchologist of the soul.»*

*xenial* — of the relationship between host and guest. *«Our meeting on the doorsill, that xenial verge, dissolved all self-absorption.»* Xenia is hospitality and the fertilizing influence pollen from one plant has on the seeds of another. The many ways that guest and host enjoy and serve each other and the new combinations that come from their company together are held in this word. *«Card tricks, ecstatic poems, looking through magazines, singing with the cello, we spread the warm Spring xenia over miles of coastline.»*

*compossible* — possible along with something else, coexisting, independent, interpenetrating developments. Coleridge in 1827 writes in his letters, "Would to God I could have made the one compossible with the other and done both." But nobody much since has used this mysterious and useful adjective, *compossible.* I'll say this. *«The presence and absence of God is compossible.»*

*cubital* — as long as the forearm. *«Spray-painted grafitti surprisingly neat and cubital.»*

*ctenoid* [The *c* is silent. Make a snakelike sneer and say TENOID]— resembling a comb, having thin, spiny teeth. *«As he replied, he leaned and felt back above his head in his characteristically ctenoid gesture.»*

*cowan* — a builder of dry-stone walls who doesn't use mortor; applied derogatively to one who practices masonry without being born to, or apprenticed in, the trade. *«In making new poems from the scholarly translations I'm given, I feel like some hermit-cowan alone in the woods building personal refuge with stones that may have once been a mill, or a church, or a bridge, no one knows.»*

*ice-blink* — the ice-cliff seafront of a glacier. *«The luminous ice-blink shivered and came after us.»*

*ing* — in the north of England a name for a meadow near a river, often part of the flood-plain. *«Inside the creek's long bend was an ing of marsh grass, which looked to be a perfect spot for a cabin.»* I wonder is there some connection between ing and England? *«Living on the ing, you know nothing's here for long.»*

*jad* — from quarry-work. A long, deep hole made for detaching large blocks from their beds. *«With crowbars they jadded behind the cornice, then tied pulling-ropes to the car bumper.»*

*terratoma* — a tumor of the earth.

*dextrocardiac* — someone with their heart in the right place. *«Let the final diagnosis be: dextrocardiac in terratoma.»*

*bobbit* — the little hopeless bit of something that *must* be found.

*davit* — a shipboard crane used for raising and lowering lifeboats, the anchor, or fish. *«Got a bobbit stuck in your davit, mate.»*

*bonaqua* — the good wet, a positive word for masturbation, a relaxed flow. *«Bon appetit, the equation came out well, bonaqua?»*

*isomer* — something very like, but in another energy state. *«I loved how in high school we sat there, isomers of something evermore about to be, what Wordsworth called April.»*

*dabuh* — the Arab word for the striped hyena.

*dacebright* — a dace is a small freshwater fish. *«The dabuh nighteyes dacebright in their desert hunger.»*

*flitch* — a strengthening plate added to a beam, a joist, or any woodwork.

*gufa* — a round boat made of straw and palm branches found in Mesopotamia. *«The oldest rivercraft in existence: the cauldron shape of a gufa crossing the Tigris.»*

*toman* — a military force of ten thousand men. A Mongol term. *«Twice ten thousand tomans died in Russia during WWII.»*

*otiose* [O SHEE OSE] — sterile, superficial, at one's ease.

*olour* — of or for swans. *«The olour feel of her neck against my wrist.»* *«The Himalayan lake too high to be visited by humans, sanctuary secret and olour.»*

*ollav* — in Irish antiquity, a master of some art or branch of learning. *«Among the O'Bryans the ollavs were poets as well as family genealogists. Now John Seawright has restored that mastery to its proper residence in a human community.»* *«Ollav at your insults!»*

*ollapod* — a sentence made of a mixture of languages. From *olla podrida,* "the rotten pot," a Spanish dish of many kinds of meats and vegetables stewed long together. *«That beautiful book of ollapods that I thought I'd never be able to read,* Finnegans Wake, *the nonce of nonciforms, grows clearer as I approach my own divine disintegration.»*

*omasum* — the third stomach of a ruminant. *«The way from wet meadowgrass to the horntips of a bull standing in the sun leads through the omasumous labyrinth, much as any idea has to come apart completely to find its application.» «The opossum needs no omasum.»*

*ombrology* — the study of rain. *«It never rains on an ombrologist's parade.» «Two amateur ombrologists risking the flu.»*

*omophore* — one who bears things on his or her shoulders. *«A strange line of headless teenage omophores lugging mattresses up the dormitory stairs.»*

*omophorion* — a kind of shawl around the shoulders worn by patriarchs and bishops out of custom rather than through any given authority.

*omophagous* — living on raw food, especially raw meat. «*The omophorians fell off as the omophagous ritual involving live goats got going.*»

*owl in an ivy bush* — a woman's birdlike features surrounded by thick disheveled hair, *à la blouse*. «*This owl in its otiose ivy looks bushed.*»

*plantad* — towards the sole of the foot. «*Hermes smiling, his attention plantad.*»

*plumous* — feathery, stuffed with down. «*She fell laughing in a plumous heap on the couch.*»

*pompkin* — a native of Boston. «*By marrying Michael Curtis, an editor of* The Atlantic, *my sister Betsy has turned into a pompkin.*»

*plangent* — making the noise of waves against the shore, relentlessly throbbing with grief. «*More eerie than poignant, his plangent calling became the wind.*»

*planish* — to make smooth and level. *«Don't planish the poem to one consistent thought.»* *«The committee's job, which it did well, was to planish contentious points and give the group a simple motion to vote up or down.»*

*randall* — a set of nonsensical verses which must be made up on the spot by schoolboys in Ireland, who have farted within earshot of their companions and who if they neglect this duty are subject to kicks, pinches, and cuffings, accompanied by diverse admonitory couplets. *«Oh the randalls began and proceeded down the standingroom bus, their noisome, moisty fuss, thickening the pall of driverly and backlook hats.»* Or, *«He randalled his way into her heart.»* Or,

> *«There was a rap artist named Randall,*
> *whose expertise was a scandal.*
> *Right with the beat,*
> *he'd crouch on the street,*
> *then fart, and blow out a candle.»*

*roger* — to lie with a woman. From the common practice of naming a bull Roger. *«Roger, what do you need? Roger?»*

*cundum* — the dried stomach of a sheep, used by men in the act of coition to prevent disease. Also the oil-skin case for holding the colors of a regiment. Said to have been invented by a Colonel Cundum. «*I know what you're after, cully cundum; you're after my laughter.*»

*cully* — dumb.

*pelsy* — trivial and trashy. «*A slight and pelsy meal retrieved from garbage cans.*»

*passulate* — to make into raisins. «*He could take and passulate the juiciest day with his worry and regulations, still sweet maybe, but greatly diminished.*» Or it could be positive: «*The long talking so passulated and condensed their desire that each gave up keeping a journal, and sex was very different.*»

*snoach* — to speak through one's nose, or with one's fingers blocking the nose.

*slamkin* — one whose clothes seem hung on with a pitchfork.

*snudge* — a thief who hides under the bed to rob the house when everyone's asleep. *«So the mother slamkin in her motley nightrobes snoached a mock-warning, "All you under-the-bed monsters, time to go back to your swamps and caves," not guessing the snudge was actually in place.»*

*palingman* — one who deals in eels. *«Beyond doubt, the free and most elusive, impeccable of point, the palingman of poetry, Bill Stafford.»*

*oe* — Gaelic for grandchild. *«My eppidoodle oe, smiling from the water like a sea urchin.»*

*opisthodomos* — an apartment at the back of a Greek temple corresponding to the vestibule at the front. *«My thoughts in church, always opisthodomal.» «Even in winter I loved to sleep out in the weather on the back porch, my opisthodomos, my mystery.»*

*gibbijen* — a stopwatch found hanging
   inexplicably from a limb in the deep
   woods. *«Simply because it was* there,
   *they couldn't see the gibbijen at first; then
   they both did, and amazingly, it was*
   working, *timing the fall.»* Someone
   or something so out of place as to be
   almost invisible.

*borborigmie* — gurgling drips and basement
   pipe-rushings heard through
   a stethescope held to a belly.
   *«Borborigmie sounds like skinny noodles
   with shrimp.»*

*obturate* — to close up an opening, to
   stop the flow. *«He called himself "the
   temporary obturator," having been hired
   to plug the leak.»*

*nouricery* [NOURISH-ERY] — a place where
   growing things are loved and tended.
   *«The smell of food being cooked, curry,
   and Indian music playing, made the door
   a nouricery for all who happened by.»*

*nitor* — dark brilliance and clarity. *«She
   seemed transparent against the nitor of an
   amber sky.»*

*pignorate* — to give as a pledge, to pawn. «*He was carrying a hairdryer, a rusty eggbeater, and a brokenwinged toaster, as the paltriest pignorations possible.*»

*perlustrate* — to go round and view, to survey completely. «*When they came to the icon of Andrew the Fool, perlustration began.*»

*wibling's witch* — from James Wibling, who, whenever he held the four of clubs in his hand, whatever the game, he won, so that card came to have a nickname. «*From under the flitch that held the split tableleg together he slid his wibling-witch ace of hearts.*»

*discerebrate* — to deprive of the brain, to disbrain. «*His loud entrance discerebrated conversation.*»

*dirhombohedron* — a double six-sided pyramid whose faces are identical isosceles triangles. «*Nerds in their subtle dirhombohedrons never win the Soapbox Derby.*»

*drix* — the rotten part of wood. «*He easily pried loose the drix with one finger and looked back at me.*»

*drury* — sexual love, often illicit. *«Dreary drury, the exhausted music of limbo.»*

*epipterous* — of seeds that have wings. *«Epipterous sycamores releasing their flocks.»*

*epirot* [EPPY-ROT] — belonging inland, the opposite of maritime. *«Local color epirots with no oceanic urge.»*

*dishelm* — to deprive someone of his helmet, or to take off one's own. *«He stood before her, dishelmed and forgiven.»*

*disheir* — to stop the lineage of. *«The villain stopped in mid-swing, "I give you the pleasure of disheiring the captain."»*

*dimble* — a rough-wooded dip in the ground, a dell.

*exergastic* — an obscure, but expansive, rhetorical figure mentioned in Puttenham's *English Poesie* as being derived, somehow, from the work of marble-polishing. "We abide in one place and yet seem to speak several different things, many times repeating one sentence, yet with other words, sentences, and ornaments." *«To escape the exergastic afternoon, we headed for the dimble.»*

*backslang* — a kind of familiar talking where words are pronounced in reverse: *look* is *cool, dog* is *God,* and *you* are *uoy.*

*aliry* — across each other. «*In the hayride truck the great soft circle sang, legs all aliry.*»

*feezy* — worried, mildly confused and alarmed. «*Much of her feezy life she spent paging McCall's and smoking Chesterfields, waiting for ominous news.*»

*unjealous* — to free of jealousy. «*He had somehow unjealoused himself, and all around felt giddy.*»

*breccia* — gravel, pieces of angular rock fragments loosely held in sand or lime, the opposite of conglomerate. «*Over the next five years his determined afflatus gave the local breccia dragonform, a wall sometimes twenty-five feet high and four feet thick, uncoiling through the woods behind his suburban ranch façade.*»

*bosset* — a small protuberance, or knob. «*The Olympic swimmers took the platforms for the two hundred free, goggled and barely suited at all, seven bossets in a row.*»

*botts* — the larvae of a parasite inhabiting
the digestive organ of the horse;
also found under the skin of cattle,
a gadfly, and in the frontal sinus of
sheep. Humorously applied to a
bowel complaint in people. *«Go off
now with your casseroles! That last year
gave me the botts,* ad infinitum.*»*

*arval* — supper served after a funeral. *«I was
numb until the arval when the custom of
his long, generous blessings fell to me.»*

*arundinous* — reedy. *«Four a.m., the night
arundinous with longing.»*

*jelarm* — a playful nickname for the identity
that pilgrims share as they approach
the truth. *«Jelarm, jelarm, they walked
along singing. Who's tending the farm,
jelarm? Honored traveler on the way with
us.»*

*bryology* — that branch of botany which
studies moss.

*bryony* — a wild vine with white flowers.
*«Bryan in the bryony.»*

*bucentaur* — a very ornate, gilded, besculptured boat with the figurehead a creature half-man, half-ox. It was used only on Ascension Day to take the Doge of Venice to wed the Adriatic by dropping a ring into the sea. *«The beige Buick convertible was ceremonial, a bucentaur driven to the beach in mid-April for his perennial re-tasting of saltwater.»*

*bucinnatory* — having to do with trumpeting, or whistling. *«Roy could be heard always before he was seen, out on his grand bucinnatory strolls.»*

*thingamabubba* — the computer-generated "official" mascot for the Atlanta Olympics in 1996.

*stang* — the rail used to ride someone about town in public humiliation, a popular extra-legal form of punishment, as for wife-beating, in the middle ages and later.

*staminody* — the metamorphosis from any flower-organ, as a petal or sepal, into a stamen. *«He had ridden their stupid village stang long enough. Now his locomotive staminody eases out from under the trees onto open prairie.»*

*hachure* — a line used for shading, as on a map to indicate mountains. *«Long hachures down the cliff in full sunlight, guy-lines for attack being daringly drawn.»*

*bonne-bouche* — a tasty morsel kept for last, so as to finish with a "good (taste in the) mouth."

*glans* — Latin for acorn, the head of the penis or of the clitoris. *«Glans are us, bonne-bouche.»*

*foveola* — a small pit, from fovea, the depression in the yellow spot on the retina. *«Each duck rode its private foveola on the rainy lake.»*

*fouraggere* [FOR-RAH-ZHAIR] — An ornamental cord worn on the shoulder, originally for a mounted man to bind forage with to the saddle. Now an honorary decoration.

*crapulous* — Sick from overeating and drinking, excessively nauseous. *«Crapulous, yourselfulous, I feel fine.»*

*cramoisy* — heraldic crimson.

*bezonian* — a raw recruit, someone in
 need of everything — instruction,
 equipment, and rations. A word
 Shakespeare made up from the Italian,
 *bisongno,* want. «*Seventh graders, you
 loud, skinny bezonians, I see your glory.*»

*bice* — a blue-green, coppery color. «*A line of
 tiny fish, bice and cramoisy, slung a lovely
 fouraggere around my arm.*»

*dipsas* — the fabulous snake whose bite
 causes a mortal thirst.

*gnomonics* — the art of dialing, from
 gnomon, the triangular plate used
 to cast a shadow on a marked dial-
 surface to indicate the hour. «*We trod
 the bosky spine of Avebury, that great
 gnomonic dipsas at the end of a terrifying
 drive on the wrongside.*»

*trilby* — A soft felt alpine hat, or in the
 plural, feet. «*She slipped the clothes off
 him, trilby to trilbies, no complaints.*»

*onsene* — the countenance. «*Dare look
 through the onsene's eyes into the mirror
 and back to source.*» «*Onsene rain, I taste
 you.*»

*privity* — the condition of being private and secret, though in fellowship with natural, even divine, companions.

*oology* — the study of bird eggs. *«The oologist walked straight through the house to the dense hedge behind and began scanning its tangle of text.»*

*onychomancy* [ONNY KO MANCY] — divination through examining the lines and quartermoons and ridges of the fingernails.

*tiromancy* — divination using cheese.

*onygophagist* [ONNY GO FOGGIST] — one who bites his or her nails. *«Practicing tiromancy and onychomancy simultaneously, I predict, will lead to tirophagy, if not the other.»*

*peepeye* — recognition. *«The only airplane baby played most godly peepeye with whoever would.»*

*naufrage* — a shipwreck. *«Naufraged and strangely happy, he lay back on the wreckage and slept.»*

*naumachia* — a mimicry of a sea battle. *«The War Room had a Persian Gulf set with model ships in childish naumachias.»*

**nauphial** — of a larval stage in lower crustaceans characterized by an unsegmented body, an unpaired median eye, and three pairs of legs. *«With her walker and her patience she looked out her one window with nauphial expectancy.»*

**naupegical** — of shipbuilding. *«Like the man on his desert island, I am beginning to feel chronic and slightly naupegical.» «He had suppressed reaction to his wife so long it was bound to erupt in a grandiose, naupegical scheme.»*

**nautch** — an East Indian dancing girl. *«Let's bring this chorus line up a nautch.»*

**neal** — of water, deep and profound. *«In the forest well, neal with golden fish and snakes.»*

**nemoral** — frequenting, or living in, groves. *«They were friends in intimate, nemoral ways.»*

**neophron** — the white Egyptian vulture.

**neomenia** — the time of the new moon, and of the festivals held at the start of the lunar month. *«The quiet peace of a neomenial desert dawn, neophron waiting for noon.»*

*pellicle* — a fine layer that reflects light, a filmy membrane, the thin scum on a liquid. *«Each juice in its own pellicle, frames for the home movie.»*

*orogeny* — the process of building mountains by the folding and faulting of the earth's crust.

*marcessent* — dead but not yet fallen off. *«Her arm marcessent in the yellow light turning the album page.»*

*gryllus* — a legendary combination of animals, face of Sophocles, rump of goat, comb of parrot, fish scales on his back, who could change into other combinations.

*syzygy* — a lining up of the sun, moon, and earth, a union of two poetic rhythms into one. *«Astronomy, poetry, seismology, and gardening, the gryllus of his many enthusiasms stalked the world, unkempt alchemical syzygy.»*

*sipapu* — Hopi, the hole in the floor of a kiva from which the ancestors emerge into the present.

*splo* — homemade liquor. *«Enough splo, the sipapu opens and visitors arrive.»*

*sipe* — the small hook-shaped groove
in the side of tire tread that gives
extra traction and prevents skidding.
*«Orogeny in the care of sipe-like fissures.»*

*deckle* — the rough untrimmed edge of
bookpapers.

*gematria* — a word whose letters have
cryptic cabalistic value.

*grumous* — a grume is a clot of blood. So,
resembling a thick fluid clustered with
granules. *«We depend on a single sipe
staying unmuddied, and the grumous,
deckled nameplate of Fruehof three feet
away, that gematria.»*

*formicary* — an ants' nest.

*cataphract* — a suit of armor for the whole
body.

*peen* — to bend or flatten as with a hammer,
to work the surface of metal with a
stream of shot. *«Her direct questions
peened his cataphract more tightly shut.
There was no way to dismantle or leave
his archaic defenses, except to starve and
be carried through the chinks by ants to
the formicary.»*

*musta* — the raw aggressive energy young bull elephants feel that makes them run hundreds of miles butting each other and trampling small trees. *«When the tornadic musta hit, we scattered to California, Oregon, Alaska, nineteen, brakes screaming steel on steel, no pads.»*

*murrey* — mulberry-colored.

*puntilla* [POON TEEEYA] — the dagger used to sever the bull's spinal cord in bullfighting. *«The puntilla went in, scintillating, came out murrey.»*

*pawky* — lively, uninhibited, canny and bold. *«At seventy-two she was rollerblading down the boardwalk at night singing Scottish ditties, pawky and Presbyterian.»*

*pleroma* — plenitude, the fullness of being, eons as well as the uncreated monad or dyad they descend from. *«Pulsant pleroma, I trust you. I might as well.»*

*inquiline* — an animal that lives in a nest made, or a hole hollowed out, by others. *«We live like the inquiline possum of an attic, walking the dark of where he is, dreaming chandeliered regions closed off.»*

*chamfer* [CAMPHOR] — a beveled edge.

*catenary* — the curve assumed by a flexible cord hanging freely from two fixed points at equal heights.

*cark* — to vex, to worry.

*sordaria* — dung-inhabiting fungi.

*sopite* [rhymes with *bite*] — to lull, to put to sleep, to resolve a claim. «*A catenary of gold cord hung across her chamfered breasts, sopiting his jealousy.*»

*grimoire* — a magician's book for invoking demons and dead spirits. «*Sordaria carking the grimoire.*»

*epergne* [EE PURN] — a large glass or silver centerpiece for a dining table with many unfolding branches and compartments for sauces and condiments.

*frass* — the excrement of larvae, or refuse left behind by boring insects. «*Cheez, the frass, it must be Spring.*» «*Even on the epergne, a film of frass.*»

*frasier* — the strawberry plant, its primrose-like flower in particular, as it decorated the Frasier clan's device. *«Adorable frasiers vining one black stocking.»*

*futhorc* — the runic alphabet, an anagram of the first six letters, f, u, th, a, r, k.

*gallet* — a rounded beach pebble. *«I suddenly realized that the gallet in my hand was the missing member of the futhorc.»*

*gasconade* — adolescent narrative exaggeration that lets the teller seem more heroic than usual. *«The gasconade continued, football exploits from the 1950's, in which the corroborating fellows were either dead, temporarily altzhammered, or willing to go along with a lie, if they could add their own.»*

*purfling* — an ornamental border, especially the inlaid edging on a violin soundbox. *«The rough purfling of the Connemara shore.»*

*fussefall* [FOOSA-FALL] — to prostrate oneself at a sovereign's feet.

*fogdom* — a region where nothing is clear. *«As a recent immigrant to fogdom, I filled my throat with it and did full fussefall at the throne.»*

*flaughen* [FLAH YEN] — a flake of flame or snow. *«The flaughens of this fire rise whirling and float back like snow, both love.»*

*flaughtbred* — with arms spread out like the wings of a bird, eager and ecstatic. *«A dervish bows beside the old sheikh, who bends and whispers, and the young man's arms open. Flaughtbred, the turning flowers out.»*

*fomalhaut* — Arabic, "the mouth of the fish," a bright star in the constellation, Southern Fish.

*footle* — silly and trifling talk. *«I can't read mystical poetry. It seems like so much footle.» «Don't play with your footle.» «How far is it from footle to fomalhaut? Those are the dimensions we're working with.»*

*danforth* — to advise of the right to refuse life-sustaining medical care. *«Has she been danforthed in 251? Well, go forth and danforth yee.»*

*fescinnine* — from an Etruscan region
notorious for lecherous songs.
Licentious, scurrilous. *«I have seen
Shakespeare changed to shallow
fescinnine fantasy.»*

*qayuqhak* [KWA YOU KWAHK] — Eskimo, for
a snowdrift shaped by the wind to
look like a duck's head. *«For years to
celebrate synonyms and particularity,
writing teachers have told students that
eskimos have two hundred words for
snow, snow floating on water, frost that
forms inside houses on clothes and boots,
snow just beginning to melt, but nobody's
given a flying qayuqhak what they were.»*
I'm told Australian aborigines have a
lot of ways to say hole.

*umbo* — the sharp point at the center of
a shield. *Umbonal,* like an umbo. *«A
handsome umbonal formation rising from
the saltflat.»*

*znees* [ZEN-EASE] — a layer of frosty ice. *«I
poked at the znees on my windshield till
it slid off in great sections.»*

*dipterist* — a studier of winged insects. *«Such
elegant purfling on the cicada.»*

*tabanids* — horseflies and deerflies that suck blood.

*torus* — a smooth protuberance on a body part. «*Tabanid on torus, making another.*»

*tarlatan* — a sheer cotton fabric in open plainweave used for dust covers. «*Throw your tarlatan over a dipterist and observe his reaction.*»

*cacologist* — one who examines excrement.

*festology* — the study of celebration. «*The festologist and the cacologist danforthed each other in the vestibule.*»

*bourock* — small heap of stones. «*A bourock, like the Great Pyramid, makes a place intentional, not to say what for.*»

*boustrophedon* — ox-turn-poetry, going right to left then left to right like a field being plowed, calligraphic, Spring-wind, slow-purposeful meandering. «*Could we see it, the underworld of roots and sleek passageways is a formicary of communication, boustrophedon gone four-dimensional.*»

*felodesan* — felonious against oneself. About actions that no one but you can injure you with. «*He robbed and bent and vandalized the joy of his soul with felodesan procrastination.*» From the Latin *felo de se,* criminal to the self.

*februate* — to purge with sacrifice and prayer. The Roman festival of purification was held on February 15th. «*Sunday night was a favorite februation of theirs, the long bath, the long long.*»

*gracile* [GRAY-SILL] — slender, lean. «*Her handwriting like trained and deeply loved hounds across the page went gracile and quick and deliberate.*»

*grace-cup* — the cup passed around after the blessing has been said, or the last cup drunk before retiring. «*Accept the grace-cup as it's handed you.*»

# Index

## A Note on Sources

Most of these xenial words are in the
OED, the *Oxford English Dictionary*
(Clarendon Press, 1933, 13 vols.) Some
are from *A Dictionary of the Vulgar Tongue*
(1811), reprinted in 1971 by Follett. A few I
discovered reading Cormac McCarthy, or
others things like an article on eskimo and
aboriginal language, and five I made up:
*gibbijen, bonaqua, jelarm, tiromancy* (which
might actually mean divination using
gullible people), and *thingamabubba.*

This first edition of XENIA
was designed & composed by
Moreland Hogan at Briarpatch Press
in Charlotte, North Carolina.

The typeface is Monotype's PostScript version
of Giovanni Mardersteig's Dante, set using
Donald Knuth's TEX.

The book was printed and bound by
Thomson-Shore, Inc. in
Dexter, Michigan.

# TRANSLATIONS
## AVAILABLE FROM MAYPOP

These translations were done by Coleman Barks in collaboration with the Persian scholar, John Moyne, Head of Linguistics, City University of New York, and with other scholarly sources listed in the various volumes.

**RUMI**

*Open Secret* (Threshold, 1984) — 83pp. $9.00. A selection of odes, quatrains, and selections from the *Mathnawi,* with Introduction. Winner of a Pushcart Writer's Choice Award. William Stafford, judge.

*Unseen Rain* (Threshold, 1986) — 83pp. $9.00. One hundred and fifty short poems from Rumi's *Rubaiyat,* with Introduction.

*We Are Three* (Maypop, 1987) — 87pp. $7.50. Odes, quatrains, and sections from the *Mathnawi,* with Notes.

*These Branching Moments* (Copper Beech, 1988) — 52pp. $6.95. Forty odes, with Introduction.

*This Longing* (Threshold, 1988) — 107pp. $9.00. Sections from the *Mathnawi* and from the *Letters,* with Introductions.

*Delicious Laughter* (Maypop, 1989) — 128pp. $7.50. Rambunctious teaching stories and other more lyric sections from the *Mathnawi,* with Introduction and Notes.

*Like This* (Maypop, 1989) — 68pp. $7.50. Forty-three odes from the *Divani Shamsi Tabriz,* with Introduction and Notes.

*Feeling the Shoulder of the Lion* (Threshold, 1991) — 103pp. $9.00. Selections from the *Mathnawi,* with Introduction and Notes.

*One-Handed Basket Weaving* (Maypop, 1991) — 135pp. $9.00. Selections from the *Mathnawi* on the theme of work, with Introduction, Notes, and Afterword.

*The Hand of Poetry*, Five Mystic Poets of Persia (Omega Press, 1993) — 208pp. $12.00 Lectures by Inayat Khan and selections of Sanai, Attar, Rumi, Saadi, and Hafiz translated by Coleman Barks, with Introduction, Preface, and a Translator's Note on each poet.

*Birdsong* (Maypop, 1993) — 64pp. $9.00. Fifty-three short poems from Rumi's *Rubaiyat.*

*Say I Am You,* Poetry Interspersed with Stories of Rumi and Shams (Maypop, 1994) — 128pp. $12.00. Poetry from Rumi's *Divan* and *Mathnawi,* as well as some poems and stories by Shams himself.

## LALLA

*Naked Song,* poems of a 14th century Kashmiri woman mystic (Maypop, 1992) — 80pp. $8.00.

## SIXTH DALAI LAMA

*Stallion on a Frozen Lake,* love songs of the 17th century tantric master (Maypop, 1992) — 72pp. $8.00.

Order from Maypop: 1-800-682-8637. 196 Westview Drive, Athens, GA 30606. Postage and handling, $2.00 for the first, and $1.00 for each additional item.

## Audio Cassettes
## Available from Maypop

*Open Secret* cassette — $9.95. Coleman Barks and Dorothy Fadiman reading Rumi's poetry accompanied by Jan Keene (flute) and Shams Kairys (violin).

*Poems of Rumi* (two cassettes) — $15.95. Robert Bly and Coleman Barks reading Rumi accompanied by Marcus Wise (tablas), David Whetstone (sitar), Celso Maldanado (drum), Michael Meade (drum), and Olatunji (drum).

*Like This* cassette — $10.95. Coleman Barks reading Rumi with Hamza el-Din on oud and tar and Huzur Coughlin on ney.

*I Want Burning,* The Ecstatic Poetry of Rumi, Hafiz, and Lalla — $10.95. Coleman Barks and Zuleikha in performance in Santa Fe with Pepe Mendoza (Andean flute) and Shabda Owens (keyboard and tar).

*New Dimensions Radio Interview* — $9.00. Michael Thoms and Coleman Barks in conversation about Rumi.

*Poetry of Longing* (two cassettes — *Birdsong* and *Say I Am You*) — $18.95. Coleman Barks reading Rumi with Marcus Wise, David Whetstone, and others on tablas, sitar, flute, ceramic bowl, and other percussion.

## OTHER BOOKS
## AVAILABLE FROM MAYPOP

*Great Song,* The Life and Teachings of Joe Miller (Maypop, 1993) — 240pp, with 32 photographs. $16. Compiled, edited, and introduced by Richard Power. Preface by Coleman Barks. Joe Miller was an eclectic, ecstatic, eccentric, wholly original, homemade American mystic. He performed in vaudeville. He drove a Wonder Bread truck, and in the 1970's and '80's he led the famous Thursday Morning Walks through Golden Gate Park in San Francisco. He taught by singing and haranguing and by giving his great heart to everyone he met. These are excerpts from his talks.

*Gourd Seed* — 128pp. $9. Original poetry and short prose by Coleman Barks.

**ORDER 1-800-682-8637**

Gen 0901/4 773